# Collage

**Sally Henry**

**PowerKiDS** press

New York

Published in 2009 by The Rosen Publishing Group, Inc.
29 East 21st Street, New York, NY 10010

Editor: Alex Woolf
Designers: Sally Henry and Trevor Cook
Consultant: Daisy Fearns
U.S. Editor: Kara Murray

Picture credits: Sally Henry and Trevor Cook

Every attempt has been made to clear copyright. Should there
be any inadvertent omission, please apply to the publisher
for rectification.

Library of Congress Cataloging-in-Publication Data

Henry, Sally.
  Collage / Sally Henry.
      p. cm. — (Make your own art)
  Includes index.
  ISBN 978-1-4358-2509-3 (library binding)
ISBN 978-1-4358-2642-7 (pbk)
ISBN 978-1-4358-2654-0 (6-pack)
  1. Collage—Juvenile literature.  I. Title.
  TT910.H487 2009
  702.81'2—dc22
                                    2008004410

Manufactured in China

# Contents

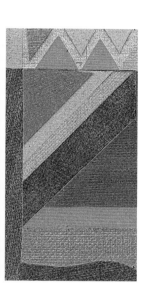

# Introduction

"Collage" comes from the French word for glue. It's all about sticking different things together to make pictures. Follow the instructions with your own choice of materials to make a one-of-a-kind artwork.

## Collecting materials

You can make your collage out of almost anything. Start off with what you might find in and around your home. Look out for color, texture and pattern. Always make sure that whatever it is you want to use, you ask first!

Here's a very short list of things to collect.

- **Colored and printed paper** – newspapers, magazines, wrapping paper, junk mail, postcards, old tickets
- **Fabric** – cloth scraps, wool
- **Plastic** – plastic bags, drinking straws, containers and lids, packaging
- **Natural things** – dried leaves, sticks, seeds, flowers, tree bark, grasses, feathers
- **Dried foods** – peas and beans, grains, pasta
- **Things from the seashore** – driftwood, shells, small stones

When you find some interesting things together in one place, you may also find that they work well together in a collage.

# Shaping your work

Cut neatly around your work with scissors. You can cut close to the edge or leave a border. Always ask an adult to help you when you are using scissors.

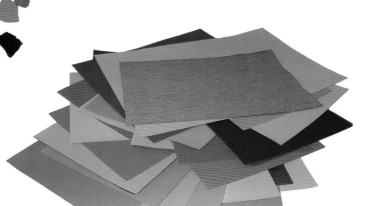

Tear paper or card stock to give a softer edge. This needs practice. Be patient and experiment! If you're tearing

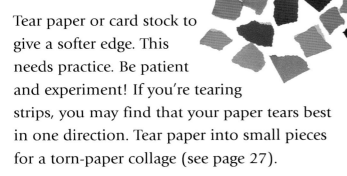

strips, you may find that your paper tears best in one direction. Tear paper into small pieces for a torn-paper collage (see page 27).

You can make very straight tears by folding and creasing the paper first. Make a tear by pulling the paper apart, holding it away from the tear line. Change your grip as you go so that you only have to pull at the point where the paper is tearing.

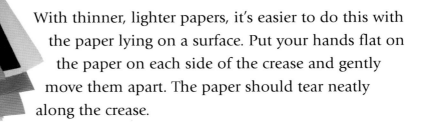

With thinner, lighter papers, it's easier to do this with the paper lying on a surface. Put your hands flat on the paper on each side of the crease and gently move them apart. The paper should tear neatly along the crease.

# Background

Try your picture on different backgrounds before you glue it down. Your background could be colored paper or card stock, posterboard or even paper plates! Box lids make excellent backgrounds for three-dimensional collage pictures. Try different shapes (see page 18).

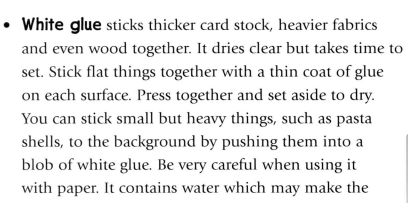

# Glue

It's important to have the right kind of glue for the material.

- **Glue sticks** are good for sticking paper and thin card stock together. Put your pieces face down on some clean scrap paper and apply glue evenly on the back. Work from the middle and spread the glue right off the edge and onto the scrap paper. Carefully put the piece in position on your artwork and press down. There should be no extra glue, blobs or mess.

- **White glue** sticks thicker card stock, heavier fabrics and even wood together. It dries clear but takes time to set. Stick flat things together with a thin coat of glue on each surface. Press together and set aside to dry. You can stick small but heavy things, such as pasta shells, to the background by pushing them into a blob of white glue. Be very careful when using it with paper. It contains water which may make the paper wrinkle.

- **Rubber cement** can come in a tube or a jar and is clear and rubbery. It's good for unusual combinations of materials. Try it with scrap before you use it on your best artwork. It tends to become stringy, and this can easily spoil your work.

# Display

Try this method for putting your work on display. Take two pieces of cardboard, each 2 x .8 inches (50 x 20 mm). Fold across the middle of each piece and bend them up a little. Use a hole punch to make holes in one end of each piece. Glue them on the back of your background board and tie string between the holes. Now you just need a hook in the wall to hang it from.

# Planning

You can start with a drawing or a photograph, or you can just put things together and see what comes to you. Try and think about the order that you'll need to do things in to get the result that you want. Remember, you're making something to keep.

# The Office Car

This project is all about looking at things in a new way. Most homes have a collection of office supplies somewhere. We've made ours into a car! What can you find? Don't forget to ask if you can have things!

## You will need:

- Colored paper, scissors
- Cardboard, silver paper
- Paper clips, an old CD
- Rubber cement
- Any small stationery items, such as clips, lids, tags, paper fasteners, picture hooks, staples, split rings

**15 MINUTES**

## What to do...

Use colored paper for the background. We've listed all the things we started with, but yours can be as different as you like. Sort out your collection and decide which things look like part of a car. Use rubber cement to hold heavier things firmly. It will dry clear.

**2 MINUTES**

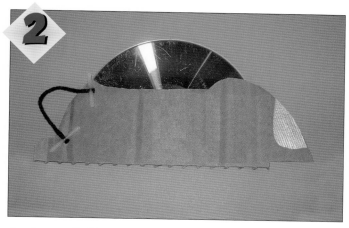

**1** Make sure no one wants the old CD before you glue it down! We only need half showing so cover the rest with the cardboard car shape.

**2** A piece of silver paper goes behind the headlight. The tag makes a good suitcase holder.

**3** The paper clips are suitcases. The bulldog clip becomes a tow bar. Put a tack on the door for a handle. Stick the plastic picture hook bar on the side panels and put the brass picture hook at the front, for a bumper.

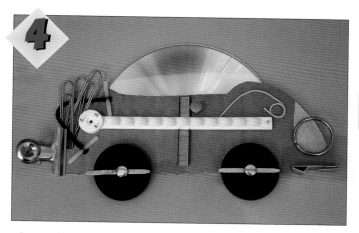

**4** The split ring is the headlamp. The wheels are plastic lids with paper fasteners opened and stuck down. We added a pink paper clip for an antenna. The office car is on the road!

## Hints and tips

• Start with something striking. These pieces of hardware have already done half the work of making a funny picture!

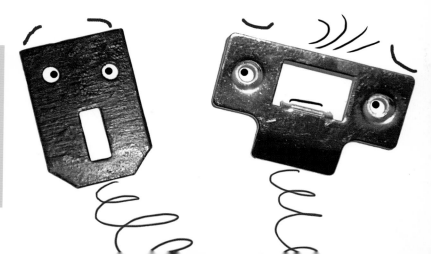

# Textures

**35 MINUTES**

**5 MINUTES**

## You will need:

- *Posterboard, scissors, glue stick*
- *Pencil, marker, paints, brush, tissues*
- *Old magazines, colored felt (optional)*

## What to do...

To create a collage like this you need to make a collection of painted or printed textures. You could even use felt or other fabrics.

Paint textures or cut out pieces of magazines.

Do a simple line drawing as a guide.

Glue the shapes onto the background.

Add figures or animals to complete your picture.

# Fun Gardening

Whatever the weather, you can make a lovely garden for yourself inside.

## You will need:

- Colored posterboard for background
- Different kinds of leaves
- Seed heads or grasses
- Flower buds, sticks
- Scissors, rubber cement
- Marker
- Wax crayons

**40 MINUTES**

## What to do...

Collect basic materials from your garden or local park. You can use dried seed heads, grasses and flowers. Even if your fresh leaves go brown, your collage will still be a beautiful tiny garden!

**5 MINUTES**

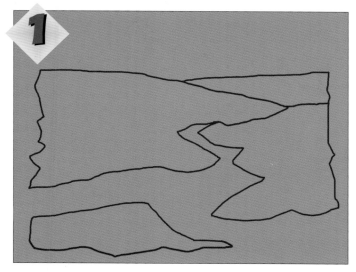

Draw simple plans for your garden as a guide to building your collage.

Arrange similar objects together to fill areas with interesting patterns and colors.

Fill in open areas with contrasting plants. Stick each piece down carefully and allow to dry.

Use special elements for trees. Leaves can make bird shapes.

## Hints and tips

- To add variety to your garden, you can use dried or pressed flowers.
- Use feathers, small shells or stones.
- The landscape on the right is done in crayons. We put in some sprigs of herbs to add interest. We think they look just like trees.

# Recycled Robot

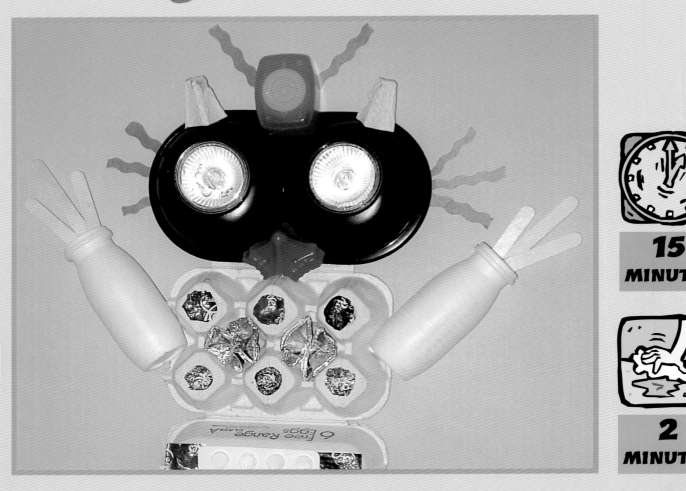

**15 MINUTES**

**2 MINUTES**

Bring a pile of bits and pieces to life! Robots are all different. Make yours now!

## You will need:

- *Colored card stock for background*
- *Rubber cement*
- *Different kinds of packaging*
- *Tin foil containers*
- *Plastic trays and lids*
- *Candy wrappers*
- *Scissors*

## What to do...

Look out for old packaging and worn-out bits and pieces that could become your robot! Ask an adult for things you can use. We found lots of the things in the recycling bin ideal for this project. Sort out what you have. Look for round things that could be eyes. Look for stringy things that could be weird hair. Arrange the pieces on your background.

Pick out the best pieces. Think about what will fit on your card stock.

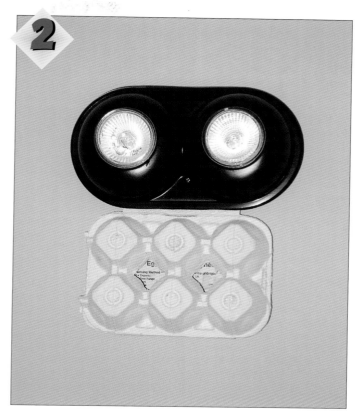

We used a plastic tray and two lids for our robot's head. His body is an egg box.

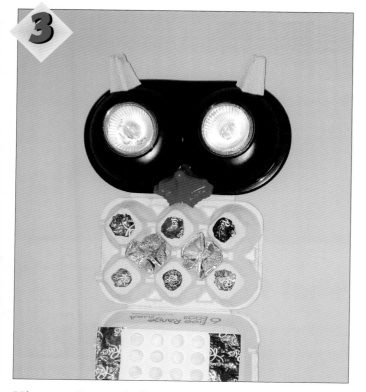

His nose is a red plastic cake tray and his ears are made of bits of egg box.

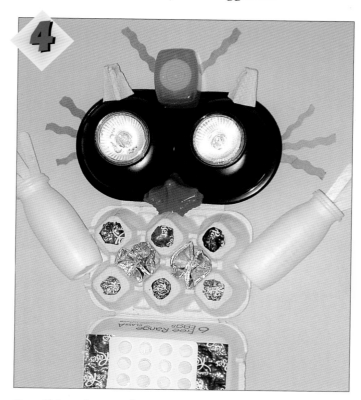

Small bottles make arms. Finally, he gets wavy cut-cardboard hair and an orange headlight!

# Pasta House

## You will need:

- Pasta shapes
- Scissors, white glue
- Poster paints and brushes
- Tissues
- Background card stock

**25 MINUTES**

## What to do...

Check the sizes of your pasta before you start painting. Make sure your house will be big enough for lots of pasta shapes.

**5 MINUTES**

Paint a simple house with a roof, walls, chimneys, windows and a door. Paint the sky blue and the grass green.

Choose some pasta shell shapes and glue them in rows along the roof. Find some pasta tubes for the chimneys.

Spiral pasta looks great over the windows and at the sides of the door. Put on more glue and find some bow-tie pasta to decorate the base.

Add more shapes to the edges of the roof and walls of the house. Use some spaghetti for the front path. It's all done!

# Fish Dinner

Here's a chance to make an appetizing meal in ten minutes! Enjoy!

## You will need:

- Paper plates
- Old magazines
- Scissors
- Glue stick

**30 MINUTES**

## What to do...

From your magazines, cut out patches of texture that remind you of food. Change the menu to suit the pictures you find.

**5 MINUTES**

Take a paper plate. We cut these french fries from a big desert picture.

The onion is a piece of a car, the mushroom is from a forest picture. The tomatoes are tomatoes!

Add the fish (it's from a jewelry picture) and a piece of lemon (from a fabric brochure).

For a dessert, try the ice cream platter (below, left) or a fruit salad!

# Making Faces

Collage is perfect for the imagination, you will soon create either a beauty or a monster.

**25** MINUTES

 **5** MINUTES

## You will need:

- Colored card stock
- Old magazines
- Scissors
- Glue stick
- Tray
- Waste basket

## What to do...

Search through your magazines for pictures of faces with eyes, noses, lips, hair, teeth and ears. You will often find them in advertisements. As you cut them out, use a tray to put the cuttings you want to keep separate from waste paper. Cut out plenty of pieces so that you will have a good selection to choose from. Use colored card stock as a background.

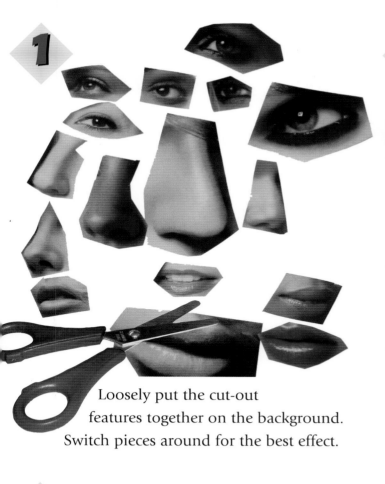

**1** Loosely put the cut-out features together on the background. Switch pieces around for the best effect.

**2** As a face starts to come together, carefully glue down the shapes. Avoid getting glue on the surface of the image.

**3** Build up the picture with pieces of skin color and hair textures.

**4** Continue to add to the collage until you are satisfied with your creation!

# Keep My Place

Never lose your place in a book again with these easy-to-make bookmarks. Copy the drawings opposite, or make up your own.

## You will need:

- White card stock, pencil
- Scissors, white glue
- Markers, crayons
- Colored paper
- Colored felt

**15 MINUTES**

## What to do...

Cut out some pieces of plain paper, about 6 x 2 inches (15 x 5 cm). Draw an animal head at the top of the card stocks. Paws, hooves or talons should reach about halfway down. Stick felt onto the back of each card stocks before you cut out the shapes.

**2 MINUTES**

Cut only
as far as
here.

23

**2** Keep your first drawing very simple. Leave a long strip
in the middle of your card, about 1 inch (25 mm)
wide. Go over your pencil drawing in black marker to
make a bold outline for the eyes, nose and mouth. Fill in
the drawing with colored markers or crayons. Cut around
the shape you have drawn. Now make two cuts on either side of
the strip to allow the legs, tentacles or flippers to hang over the
page of your book. Add extra pieces of felt to decorate your
animals.

**3** If you draw an animal with a long neck, leave
paper on either side instead of drawing paws!

Cut as
far as
here.

# Wise Owl

**40 MINUTES**

**5 MINUTES**

## You will need:

- *Colored papers*
- *Seeds or small leaves*
- *Matchsticks, felt*
- *Scissors, pencil*
- *Rubber cement*
- *Markers*

## What to do...

Choose a brightly colored sheet of paper for a background. Use cream colored paper to make the owl's body. Fold it in half lengthwise and draw the head, wing and tail shapes on your folded paper. Cut around your drawing, then unfold the shape to reveal your owl. Stick the owl's body in the middle of your background.

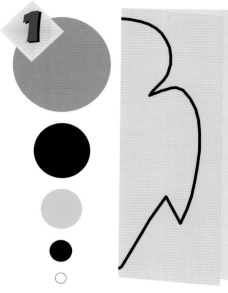

You will need ten paper or felt circles for eyes. The largest is brown. Then cut out smaller circles in black, yellow and white as shown above. Cut them out from colored paper or felt.

Stick the eyes on the head of the owl. Add pieces of matchstick around the eyes. Cut a beak shape from some orange paper. Fold it in half lengthwise and glue in place.

We have used maple seeds for feathers. You could use real feathers or small leaves. Start from the top and outer edges. Stick down each piece, overlapping as you go along.

25

Pay attention to the wings and tail. Leave the middle plain except for some little decorative touches.

Add a few feathers to his head. Cut out some claws from colored paper or felt for his feet. Glue them on.

Allow the glue to dry. Pin the work on the wall. Your first wildlife collage is finished. Good job!

# Cut and Tear

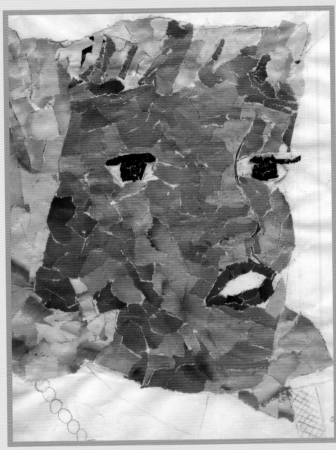

We're cutting pictures from magazines to make faces. In the collage on the left, we're using things that look like other things. In the collage on the right, we're using bits of color and texture. We tear the pictures up and use them like a mosaic.

## You will need:

- *Drawing paper*
- *Lots of old magazines*
- *Scissors, glue stick*
- *Pencil*
- *Tray*

**45 MINUTES**

## What to do...

Sort through your old magazines. Make up two collections of pictures.

**5 MINUTES**

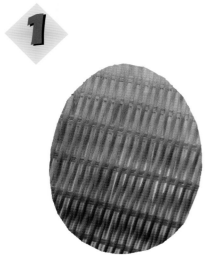

**1** Find a page with a pattern all over it. Cut out a large oval shape.

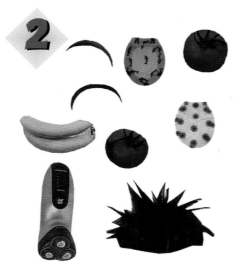

**2** Search for things that look like eyes, a nose and ears.

**3** Glue down the oval, then add the features! That's fantastic!

**1** We made our simple line drawing from a photo of a singer. Use any picture you like, but try a face first. Draw areas of different colors and texture such as eyes, the nose, lips, hair and eyebrows.

**2** Tear up lots of skin-colored printed paper from your magazines. The pieces should be about .5 inch (12 mm) square. Find other colors for eyes, hair and lips. Keep the colors in separate color groups, like a palette.

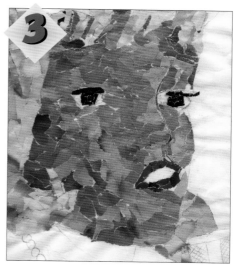

**3** Overlap the pieces as you glue them down. If you need white for eyes or teeth, allow the background paper to show. For small details, such as eyebrows or eyelashes, cut shapes from a suitable color.

# Moving Zoo

Mobiles are fun to watch and quite easy to make. They make a good present for a new baby.

**35 MINUTES**

**5 MINUTES**

## You will need:

- Colored felt, card stock
- Colored pipe cleaners, paper clips
- Black thread, sewing needle
- Scissors, fabric glue
- Tracing paper

## What to do...

You can make your own shapes or use the patterns on page 30. Trace or photocopy the animal shapes onto card stock.

**1**

Fix the animal shape to the two layers of felt with a paper clip. Carefully cut around each animal with scissors.

**2**

Stick the felt shapes to both sides of the card stock. Glue on felt stripes or spots as you wish.

**3**

Use a needle to fix 10 inches (25 cm) of thread to each animal at the place marked with a red dot on the patterns. Make ten small circles of felt or card stock for eyes and stick one to each side of the animals. Use two pipe cleaners 9 inches (23 cm) long twisted together for the top bar of the mobile. Make a hanging circle at the center.

**4**

Use one pipe cleaner to make the lower bar 4 inches (10 cm) long. Hang an animal from each end of the top bar with threads about 5 inches (13 cm) long. Hang three animals from the lower bar. Make the threads 5, 9, and 5 inches (13, 23 and 13 cm) long so the center animal hangs lowest. Use a 4-inch (10 cm) piece of thread to fix the lower bar to the top bar. Ask an adult to help you to hang the mobile.

**Elephant**

**Lion**

**Crocodile**

**Giraffe**

**Hippopotamus**

## Hints and tips

- If you are making different animals, use a pin to find the balancing point shown by the red dot on the patterns above.

# Glossary

**cardboard**  (KAHRD-bord)  Boxes for packaging are made of cardboard. It's often dull gray or brown.

**containers**  (kun-TAY-nerz)  Things that hold things.

**contrasting**  (KON-trast-ing)  Not alike.

**crease**  (KREES)  A crease is the mark left by folding paper and flattening it out again.

**fabric**  (FA-brik)  Cloth.

**grip**  (GRIP)  A firm hold.

**hook**  (HUK)  Something curled at one end and used for hanging.

**materials**  (muh-TEER-ee-ulz)  What something is made of.

**mobile**  (MOH-beel)  A mobile is an artwork that can move. It's often made to hang from the ceiling. It can be hung over a baby's crib.

**mosaic**  (moh-ZAY-ik)  A picture or pattern made of small pieces of colored glass or pottery.

**palette**  (PA-lit)  This is a tray or board for mixing paints. It can also mean the range of colors that you are using.

**pipe cleaner**  (PYP KLEE-ner)  It used to be used to clean smokers' pipes. Now there are colored ones for craft work.

**staple**  (STAY-pul)  A wire fastener you use to fix paper together.

**texture**  (TEKS-chur)  How something feels when you touch it.

**tracing paper**  (TRAYS-ing PAY-per)  Thin but strong paper you can see through. Put it on top of something you want to copy and draw on it.

# Index

# Web Sites

Due to the changing nature of Internet links, PowerKids Press has developed an online list of Web sites related to the subject of this book. This site is updated regularly. Please use this link to access the list:
www.powerkidslinks.com/myoa/collage/